To Annika and Elsa,
Idahoans on the move
DE

To the widows
JS

This book was aided by the input of the Young Editors Project,
a program that invites young readers to see manuscripts in progress.
The author would like to thank the fourth-grade students in Heather Rader's
Olympia, Washington, classroom, and Zuleikha Hester's third-grade students
Anya, Abbey, Katie, Mei, Ritika, and Roya in San Diego, California.

Many thanks to Rebecca Cox and all at the Blaine County Historical Museum
for their kindness and scholarship.

First edition 2023

Library of Congress Catalog Card Number 2022907033
ISBN 978-1-5362-1588-5

23 24 25 26 27 28 CCP 10 9 8 7 6 5 4 3 2 1

Printed in Shenzhen, Guangdong, China

This book was typeset in Bentham.
The illustrations were created digitally.

Candlewick Press
99 Dover Street
Somerville, Massachusetts 02144

www.candlewick.com

MOVING the MILLERS' MINNIE MOORE MINE MANSION

A true story

by **Dave Eggers**

illustrated by **Júlia Sardà**

CANDLEWICK PRESS

LIKE all of the best stories, this takes place in Idaho.

In the 1870s, prospectors roamed Idaho looking for gold and silver. In Bellevue, a small town in the bottom half of Idaho, they found silver.

Actually, one of the most important finds of all wasn't found by a human. It was found by a dog.

This particular dog was chasing a particular gopher around when the gopher ducked into a hole—probably his home.

The dog did not give up there, though.
He dug and dug into the gopher hole,

but instead of finding the gopher,
he found silver.

Word of the silver spread far and wide, and the small hole
the gopher made turned into a much larger hole made by men.
The man who owned the mine was named John "Minnie"
Moore, so it became known as the Minnie Moore Mine.

John
"Minnie"
Moore

A few years later, a man from England—which was, and is, an island nation quite far from Idaho—arrived and bought this land where the dog had chased the gopher, the Minnie Moore Mine. The man who bought the mine was named Henry Miller, and he hoped the mine would still be full of silver and would make him rich.

Henry
Miller

He was not wrong. He got so much silver out of what started as a gopher hole that he had all the silver he needed and became one of the wealthiest men in England or Idaho or both combined.

We can assume that the mine was then known as

Miller's Minnie Moore Mine

It only makes sense.

But Miller was alone, and he did not want to be alone.
He wanted to be married, so he went looking for a wife.

Soon he met a young woman named Annie, and they agreed to marry.

Annie had never left the country—had never left Idaho, in fact—so for a wedding present, Henry sent her to Europe, so she could see all the history and culture and food, which according to many experts was better than that which was available in Idaho in 1880.

While Annie was gallivanting about Europe—which is what you do in Europe, by the way, you gallivant; it is a kind of traipsing—Henry was determined to build his new wife a lavish new house.

When she got back, he had built her a large Victorian home in the town called Bellevue.

It was the most impressive and stately mansion for miles. It had three floors, and high ceilings, and stained glass windows. In a region where many people were still living in small shacks and even tents, this home brought a bit of Old World civility to the Old West, which was often not so civil.

The home, we can assume, was known to some, if not all, as the

Millers' Minnie Moore Mine Mansion.

WELCOME HOME, ANNIE

Henry and Annie lived there happily for years, and soon enough welcomed a son, Douglas, who played along the riverside—the house was on the riverside, mind you—and rode horses on the vast open land around the home. There is no better place for horses than Idaho. Any horse will tell you that. They are truthful animals and are especially truthful when it comes to real estate.

But sadness came to the Millers' Minnie Moore Mine Mansion.
Soon after the turn of the century, Henry died, leaving Annie
and Douglas alone.

Then things got worse. Annie was tricked by a crooked banker, who convinced her to put all her money in his bank. Then the bank went bankrupt—something banks occasionally do—and Annie and Douglas had nothing but their home.

Annie needed to find a way to make money, so she did what most of us might do in that situation: she decided to raise pigs. With her last few dollars, she bought a bunch (gaggle? herd?) of pigs and planned to breed and sell them.

But there was one catch: the town of Bellevue did not allow its residents to keep livestock in their yards.

There is, some say,
a particular smell
to cows and pigs and
sheep, and that smell
is not considered
wonderful.

So Annie had to make a choice. Either she would stay in Bellevue, in the home her beloved lost husband had built for her, or she would leave with her pigs—the only way to provide for her son.

In the end, she decided she didn't need to choose. See, your narrator just tricked you.

Annie decided to simply move the house from Bellevue to a spot just outside town, which had no prohibitions on porcine pursuits.

Your narrator just said it was simple to move the house.

But it was not simple.

It was very complicated.

Here's what Annie Miller did—with, of course, the help of her son and the workers they hired.

The house had been assembled atop a foundation made of hundreds of stones, and the first thing the workers did was to draw numbers on every one of these stones.

Why?

Don't ask why. You will learn why soon enough.

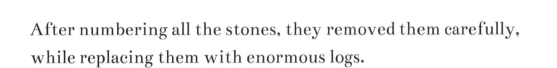

After numbering all the stones, they removed them carefully,
while replacing them with enormous logs.

Why would they replace the stones with logs?

This I can tell you right now. Because logs *roll*.

Yes. Annie Miller and her son and the workers they hired actually planned to roll the house four miles down the road, to a place where pigs were acceptable and accepted.

And this is what they did.

They placed the enormous logs under the house.
Then they attached the house to a team of horses.
And these horses pulled the house as the logs rolled underneath.

This.
Actually.
Happened.

And every time the house moved about six feet,
the workers moved the logs from the back of the
house to the front, and it all started over again.

Again and again

they rolled and replaced,

rolled and replaced.

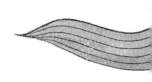

The move took about a month, and the ride was so smooth that
Annie and Douglas were able to live in the house all the while.

They.
Actually.
Did.
This.

They even had a cook, who cooked three meals a day for them,
in the house, which was rolling down the road.

The pigs, we assume, followed along behind.

When the house finally arrived at the new site, on a large plot of land by the Big Wood River—which was, and is, a real river in Idaho—the workers reassembled the stone foundation exactly as it had been before.

How?

Using the numbers they'd drawn on the stones, of course! (Idahoans are so smart.)

Then they placed the house atop the stones, and it was precisely as it had been before, only four miles away, and surrounded by pigs.

The Millers' Minnie Moore Mine Mansion stood there for
decades—in fact, it stands there today!—and Annie and
Douglas lived and thrived there for many years, as did the pigs.

Until, of course, they were eaten.

The End